Sch   D0783677

FAMOUS PEOPLE
FAMOUS LIVES

Biographies of famous people to
support the curriculum.

Beatrix
Potter

by Harriet Castor

Illustrations by Martin Remphry

W
FRANKLIN WATTS
NEW YORK•LONDON•SYDNEY

First published in 1999 by
Franklin Watts
96 Leonard Street
London
EC2A 4XD

Franklin Watts Australia
14 Mars Road
Lane Cove
NSW 2066

© 1999 text Harriet Castor
© 1999 illustrations Martin Remphry

The right of the author to be identified
as the author of this work has been asserted.

The right of the illustrator to be identified
as the illustrator of this work has been asserted.

ISBN: 0 7496 3345 X

Dewey Decimal Classification Number: 823

A CIP catalogue record for this book
is available from the British Library.

10 9 8 7 6 5 4 3 2 1

Editor: Sarah Ridley

The Original Peter Rabbit BooksTM are
published by Frederick Warne & Co.

Printed in Great Britain

Beatrix Potter

In the days when Queen Victoria was on the throne, a little girl lived on the third floor of a house in Kensington, in London. The girl's name was Beatrix Potter.

The whole house belonged to Beatrix's parents, Rupert and Helen. Like many children of wealthy families, Beatrix did not see her parents much. She lived in the nursery with her nanny.

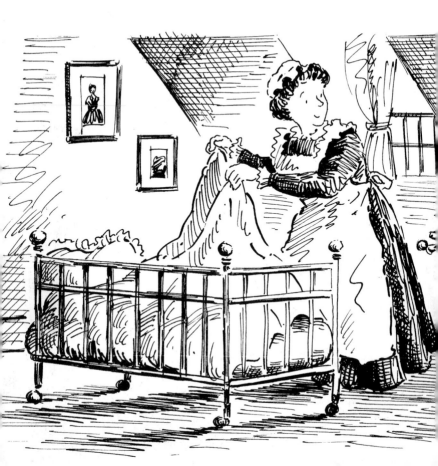

Beatrix had no other children
to play with, and because she
hardly ever met people she was
very shy. But she wasn't
unhappy. She kept herself busy.

When Beatrix was five, a baby
brother was born, called Bertram.

One of Beatrix's favourite
hobbies was drawing. She copied
pictures from books. Nearly all
her drawings were of animals
and birds.

As Bertram grew older,
Beatrix discovered that he loved
drawing as much as she did.

Every year the Potters went on a long summer holiday to Scotland. Beatrix and Bertram loved these trips. Instead of copying pictures of animals and plants, they could draw real ones.

They started collecting things they wanted to draw, like beetles and caterpillars, and the skeletons of mice and birds. They smuggled some of them back to London.

But Bertram wasn't always there to keep Beatrix company. In term-time, he was away at school. Like most rich girls then, Beatrix did not go to school. Governesses taught her at home.

As she grew up, drawing was still Beatrix's favourite pastime. She looked very carefully at the animals and plants she drew, and included every tiny detail.

Later Beatrix and Bertram collected pets. Beatrix had many animals including a dormouse, a hedgehog called Tiggy and a rabbit called Benjamin Bouncer.

Benjamin was supposed to live in the garden, but instead he spent most of his time in the nursery

and slept in front of the fire.
There were bats, too, and fish
and snails. Bertram had a falcon
and an owl.

Beatrix liked going to museums.
She sat for hours, drawing fossils
and insects. She was also very
interested in fungi and mould
which she collected on holiday in
Scotland. She used a microscope
and drew what it showed her.

Beatrix had some new ideas about fungi, and she took her drawings to the expert scientists at Kew Gardens. They didn't take her seriously, though, because she was not a professional scientist – and she was a woman.

Disappointed, Beatrix put her
fungi drawings away. Instead,
she amused herself writing letters
to children she knew, and drawing
pictures of her pets for them.

One of the children was a boy called Noel, who was ill. When she couldn't think of any news one day, Beatrix made her letter to Noel into a story. It was about her new pet rabbit, Peter.

Noel loved his letter, and so did the other children Beatrix wrote to. She told them about Squirrel Nutkin, Mrs Tiggy-Winkle and a frog called Jeremy Fisher.

Several years later, Beatrix decided that her story about Peter Rabbit might make a good book. But when she showed it to some publishers, they all said no. Beatrix didn't give up. She used her own savings to pay for the printing.

19

In December 1901 *The Tale of Peter Rabbit* was ready. Beatrix sold copies to her family and friends.

Then she showed the book again. to one of the publishers. This time Frederick Warne and Company said yes.

The Tale of Peter Rabbit was a great success. Beatrix began working on other stories.

Many stories were about her real pets, such as Benjamin Bunny and Mrs Tiggy-Winkle.

Beatrix also reared a little black pig called Pig-wig, who

appears in the story, *The Tale of Pigling Bland.*

Beatrix always drew from life. When she wanted to draw pigs, she sat *in* the pig sty!

Beatrix enjoyed her work. She became great friends with the publishers, the Warne family, especially with Norman Warne.

Mr and Mrs Potter were proud of Beatrix's books.

But, even though she was nearly forty, her parents thought an unmarried daughter should stay quietly at home. They did not like Beatrix having new friends and earning her own money.

To help with a new book she was working on, one of Norman's brothers invited Beatrix to come and draw his daughter's doll's house. Beatrix's mother said no, so Norman sent her photographs of it instead.

Later, though, Beatrix did manage to visit Norman's brother. She studied the doll's house and borrowed a policeman doll. You can see her drawings of them both in *The Tale of Two Bad Mice*.

In 1905, Norman Warne asked Beatrix to marry him. Beatrix was delighted. But her parents were furious. Unlike them, Norman worked for his living. To her parents this meant he was not from the right social class.

Beatrix wanted to please her parents – but she wanted to marry Norman more.

Beatrix wore Norman's ring, though she had to keep the engagement a secret.

Then, just a few weeks later, Norman fell ill and died. Beatrix was heartbroken.

Beatrix loved the Lake District. Just before Norman's death, she had decided to use the money from her books to buy a farm there, called Hill Top. She still had to live with her parents, but she visited Hill Top whenever she could.

In many of Beatrix's books – the ones about Jemima Puddle-Duck and Tom Kitten, for example – you can see Hill Top Farm and the nearby village in the pictures. You can see some of the villagers, too.

The Roly-Poly Pudding is also set at Hill Top. It's about a rat called Samuel Whiskers. When Beatrix bought Hill Top it was overrun with rats.

As the years passed, and Beatrix earned more money from her books, she bought more property near Hill Top, including a house called Castle Cottage.

Each time she bought something, the business was done by a local solicitor called William Heelis. He was tall and quiet and shy. He and Beatrix got on very well.

When William asked Beatrix
to marry him, she said yes.
She knew that her parents
would disapprove. But she was
determined they wouldn't stop
her this time.

Beatrix and Willie were married
in Kensington in 1913.
They went to live on one of
Beatrix's farms.

Now, for the first time, Beatrix could do exactly what she liked. She learned everything she could about local breeds of sheep, and won many prizes. She spent lots of time with her other animals, too – cows, hens, horses, pigs and dogs.

She did a little writing and drawing, but now she was more interested in farming than her books.

Still the books sold more and more copies. But Beatrix did not want to be famous. She was a very private person and wanted to carry on her happy life with Willie on the farm undisturbed.

She did let some fans visit her, though, especially fans from America and Australia.

Although she didn't like fame, Beatrix didn't shut herself away. She took part in village life. She was a familiar sight dressed in clogs and tweeds, checking on her sheep in all weathers. Once she was mistaken for a tramp!

Many local people loved her, though some thought she was rather fierce, since she always spoke her mind.

By the end of her life Beatrix owned a lot of land. When she died, aged seventy-seven, she left most of it to The National Trust, which a friend of hers had helped set up many years before.

Beatrix wanted the Lake District, which she loved so much and had drawn so often, to be well looked after.

She also asked that Hill Top Farm should be kept exactly as she'd left it. You can still visit Hill Top today.

Further facts

Around the world

Today, Beatrix Potter's stories are read and enjoyed by millions of people around the world. They have been translated into many languages.

All sorts of toys and games have been made using Beatrix Potter's animal characters. Beatrix started this herself; she made the first Peter Rabbit doll, and later she invented a Peter Rabbit board-game.

Code-breaking

When Beatrix was fifteen, she started keeping a secret diary. She wrote it for many years, using her own made-up code. After her death, a cousin found the diary in Beatrix's attic. The code was so difficult that it took years for anyone to break it.

Animal dances

In 1971 a new ballet was made up by Sir Frederick Ashton, the famous choreographer. It is called *The Tales of Beatrix Potter*, and all the dances are based on her stories.

Some important dates in Beatrix Potter's lifetime

1866 Beatrix Potter is born in London, the daughter of Rupert and Helen Potter.

1872 Beatrix's brother, Bertram, is born.

1893 Beatrix writes a letter to Noel Moore. It is a story about her pet rabbit, Peter.

1901 Beatrix publishes *The Tale of Peter Rabbit* herself.

1902 Frederick Warne & Co. publish *The Tale of Peter Rabbit*. The whole first printing of 8,000 copies is sold out in advance.

July, 1905 Norman Warne asks Beatrix to marry him. Beatrix says yes.

August, 1905 Norman dies, aged 37, of a type of leukaemia.

Summer, 1905 Beatrix buys Hill Top Farm in the Lake District with the money she has earned from her books.

1913 Beatrix marries William Heelis, a solicitor.

1943 Beatrix dies, aged 77.